𝕿𝖍𝖎𝖘 𝕭𝖎𝖇𝖑𝖊 𝖁𝖊𝖗𝖘𝖊
COLORING BOOK BELONGS TO

_____

_____

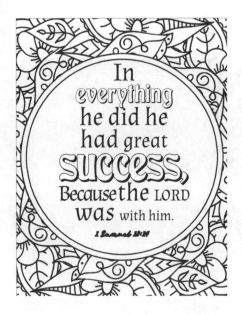

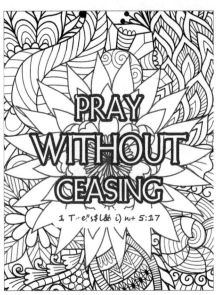

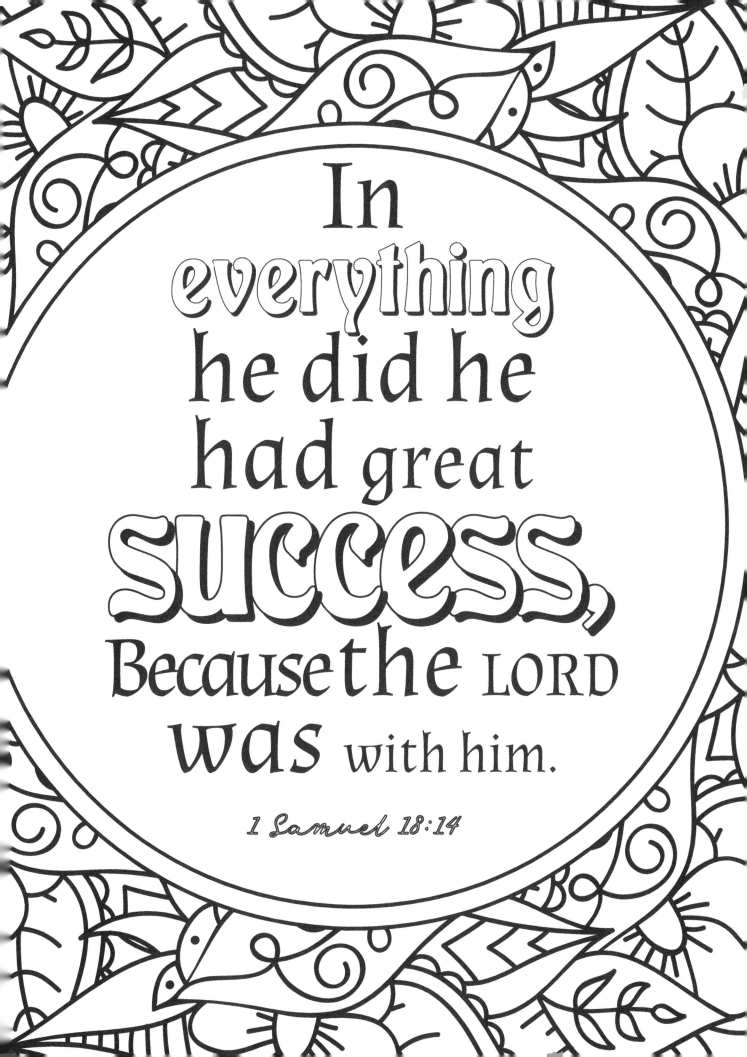

For this is the love of God, that we keep His COMMANDMENTS. And His COMMANDMENTS are not BURDENSOME.

1 John 5:3

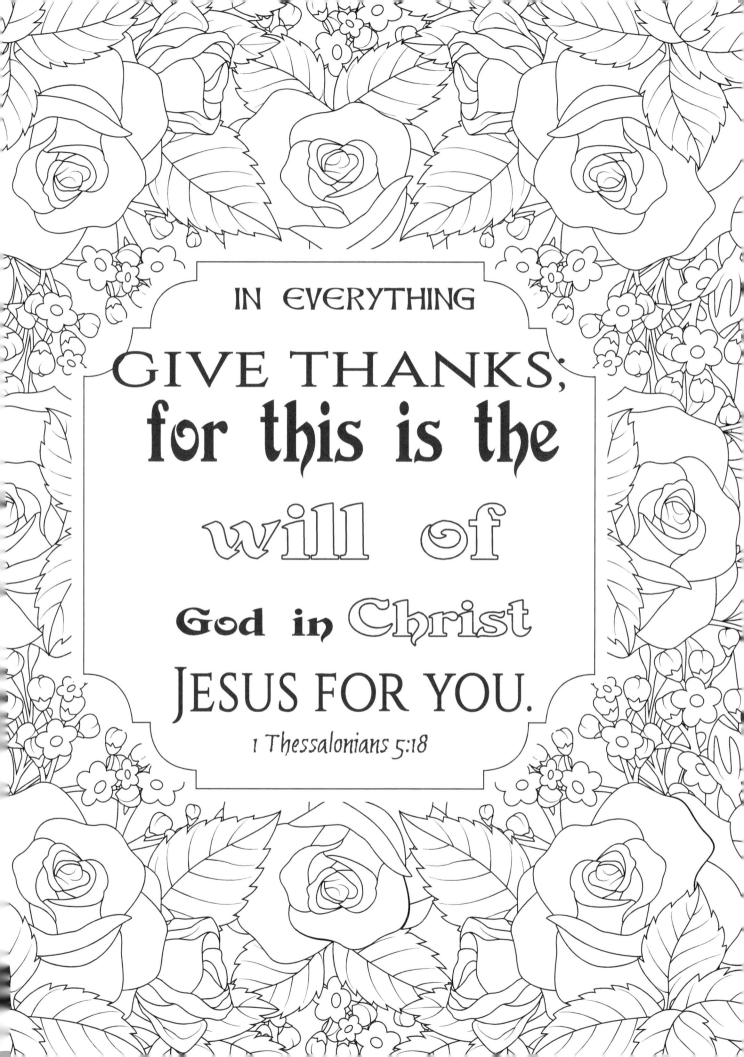

So keep the **words** of this covenant to do them, that you may **prosper** in all that **you do.**

Deuteronomy 29:9

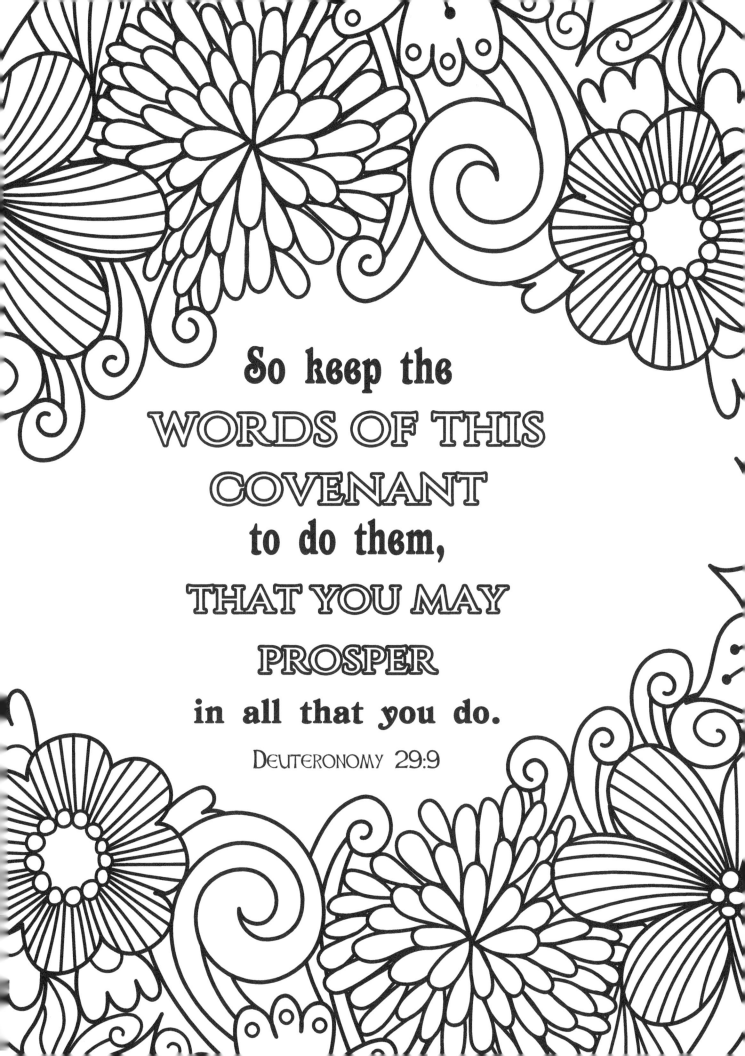

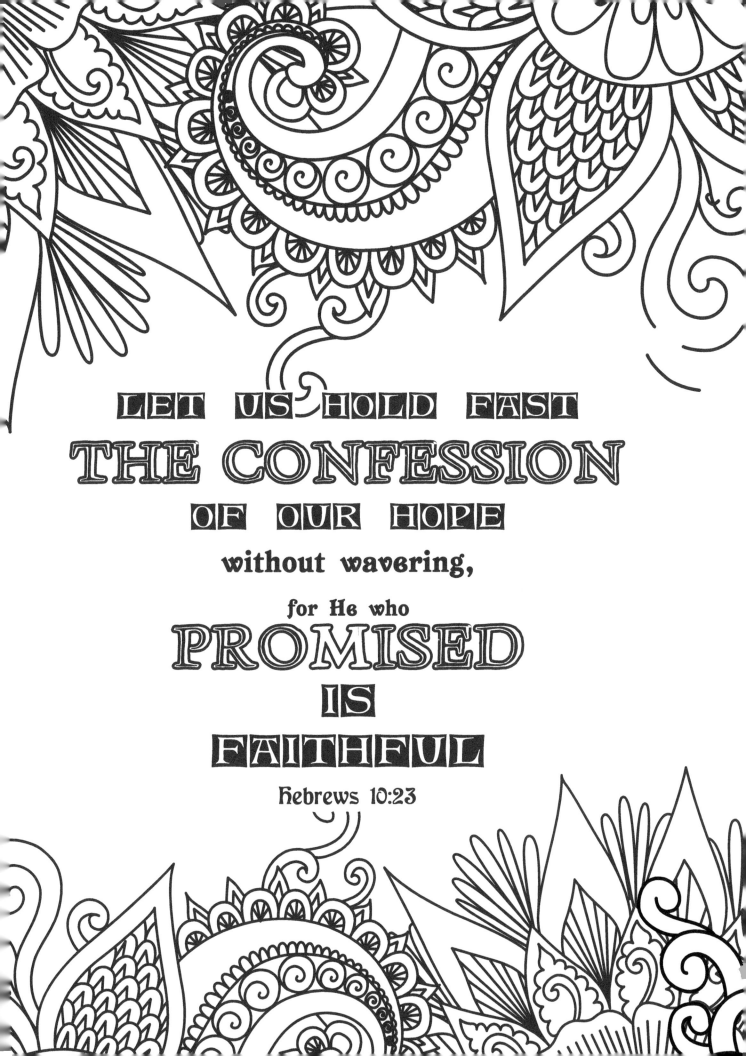

Without counsel, plans go awry, But in the multitude of counselors they are established.

Proverbs 15:22

Let the *words* of my mouth and the *meditation* of my heart Be *acceptable* in **Your Sight**

Psalm 19:14

Delight yourself also in the Lord, And He shall give you the desires of your heart.
Psalm 37:4

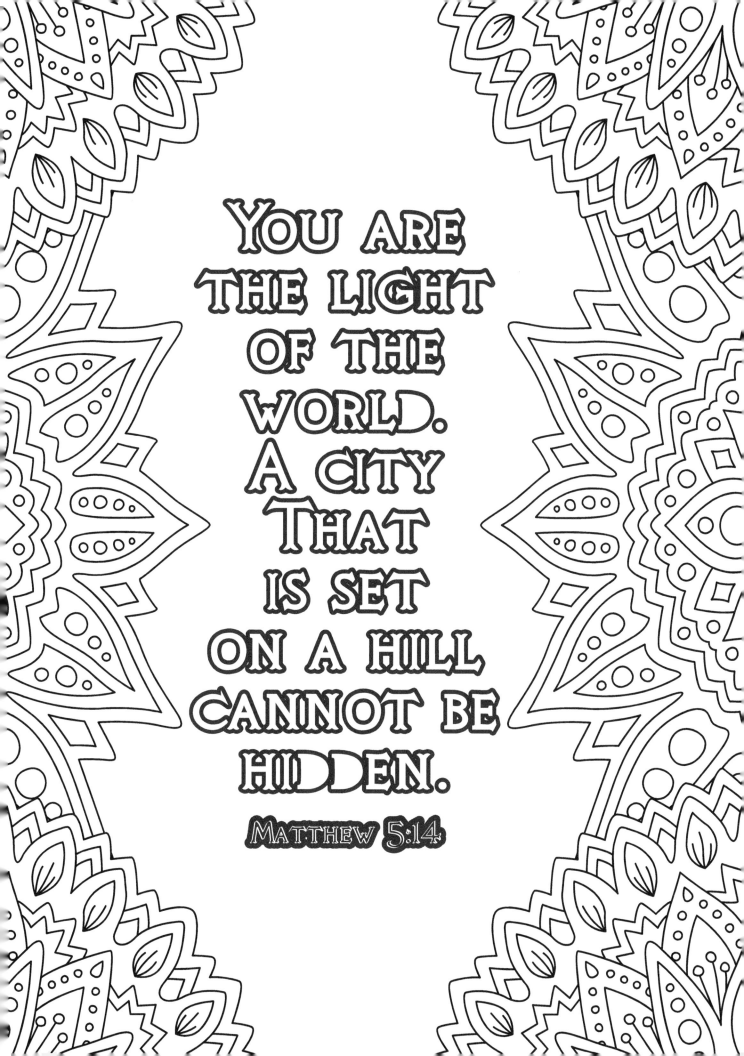

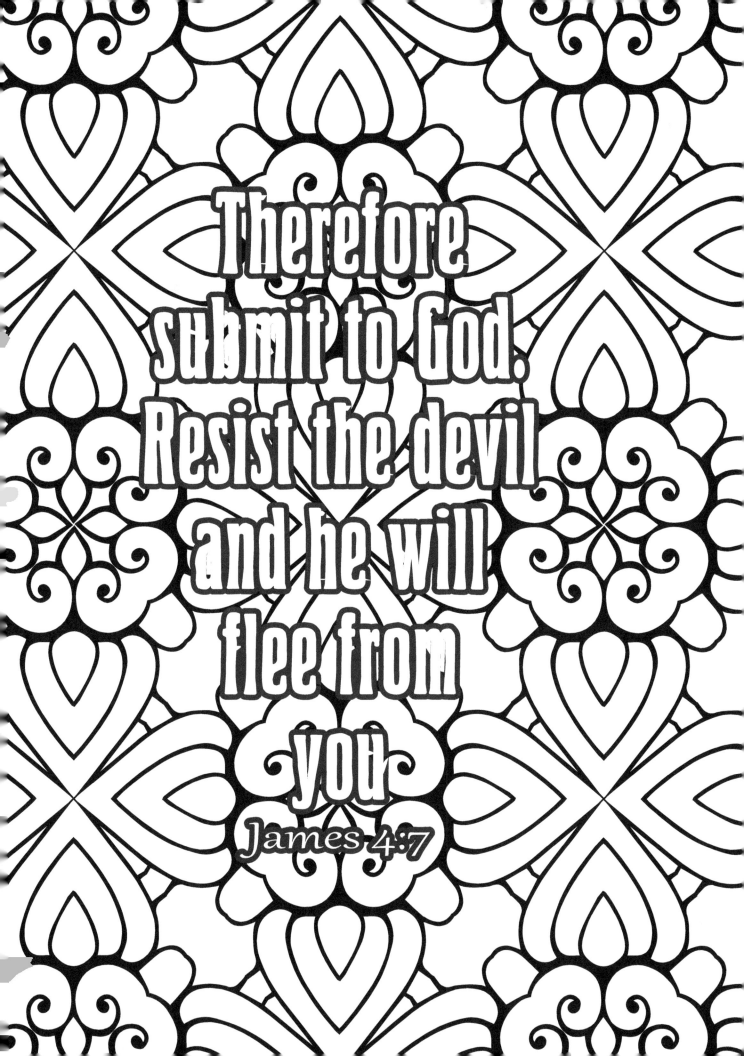

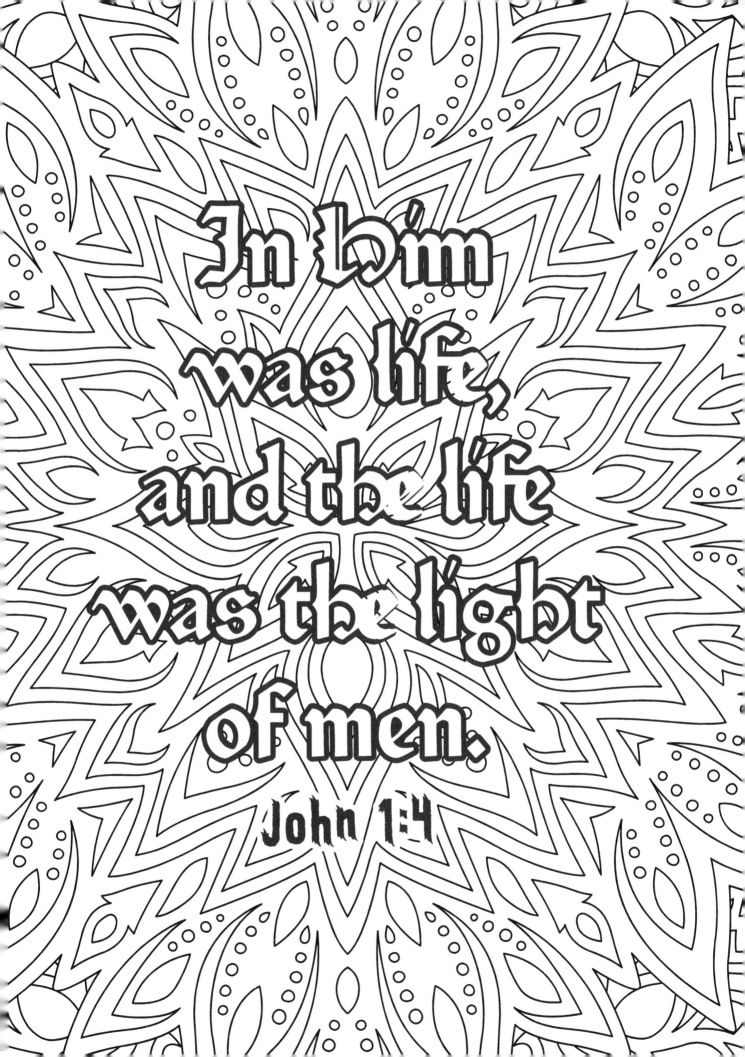

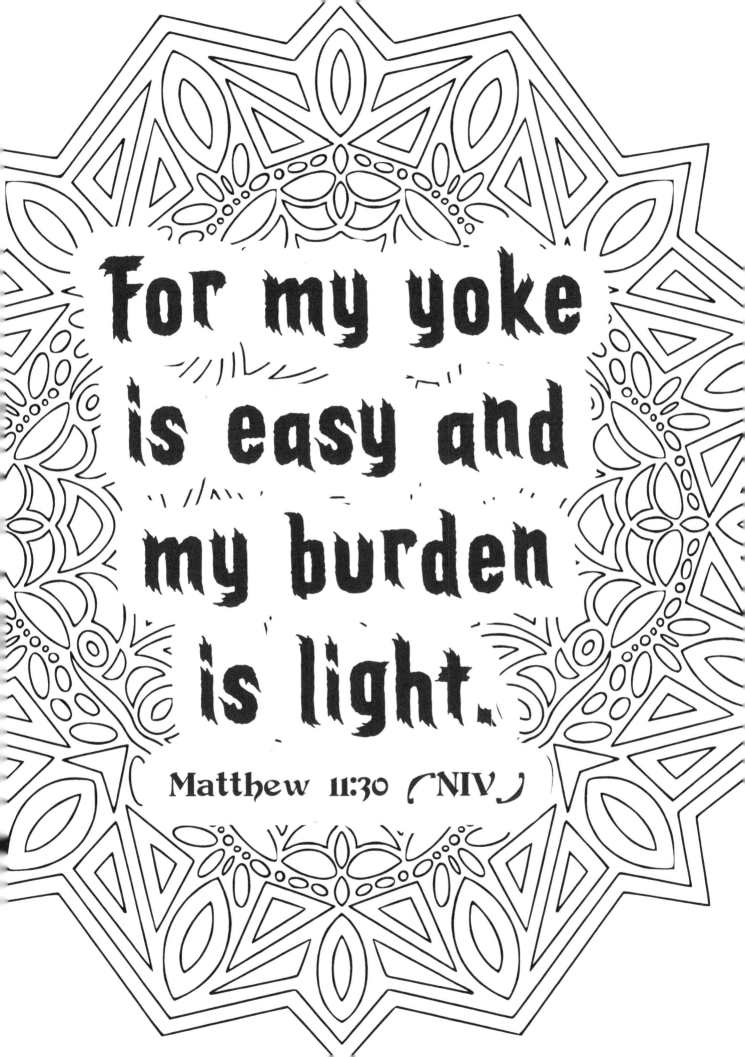

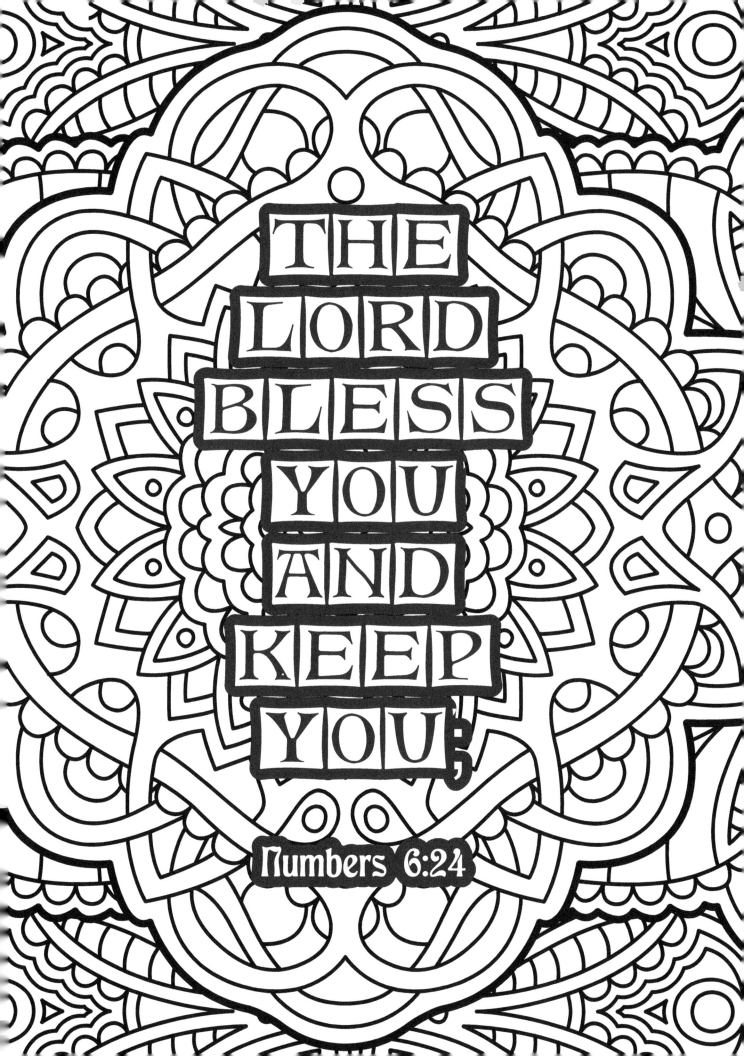

The name of the Lord
is a strong tower;
The righteous run to it
and are safe

Proverbs 18:10

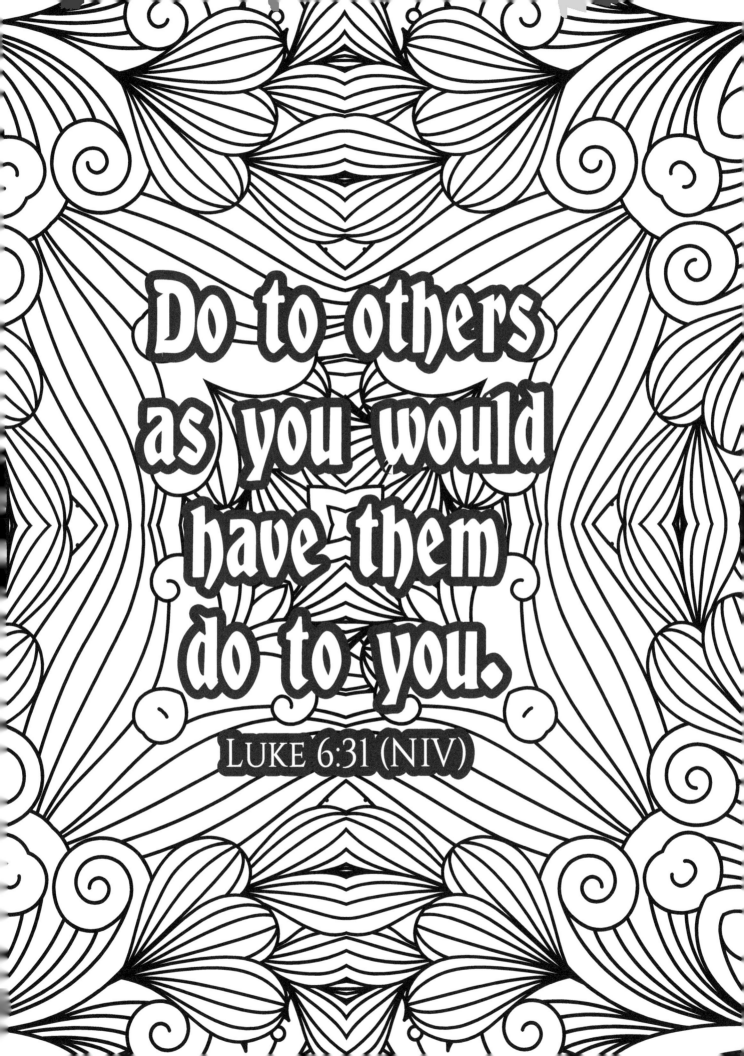

OH, GIVE THANKS TO THE Lord,
FOR HE IS good! FOR HIS MERCY
ENDURES forever.

PSALM 136:1

Commit your way to the Lord,
Trust also in Him,
And He shall bring it to pass.

Psalm 37:5

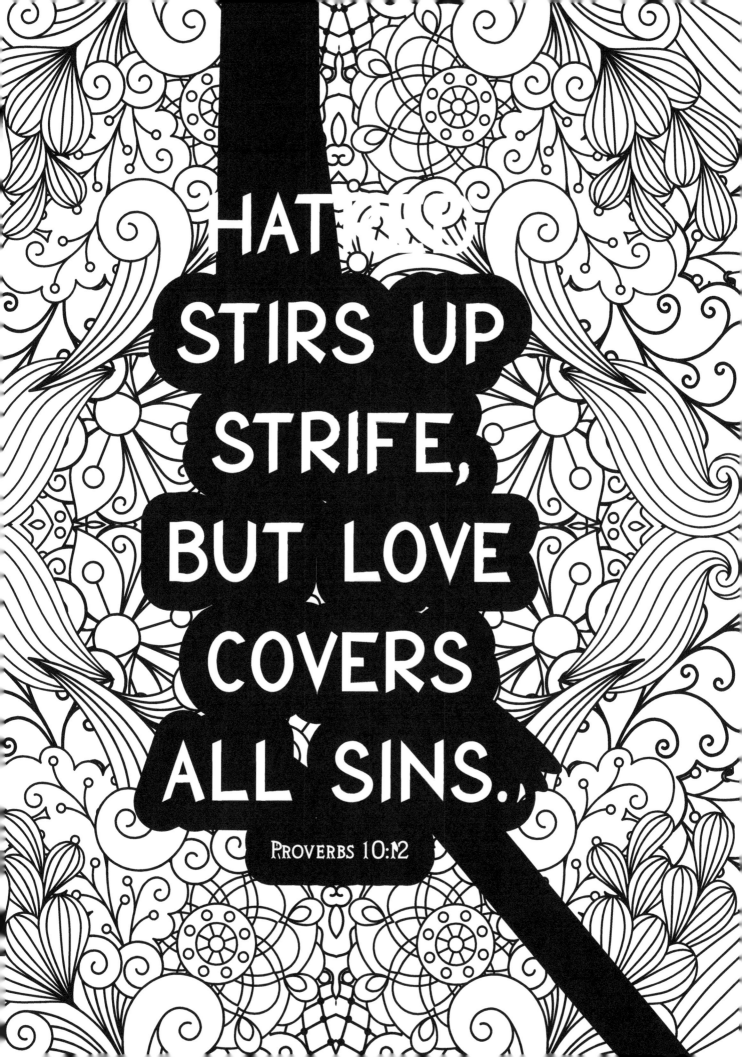

REJOICING IN HOPE,
PATIENT IN TRIBULATION,
CONTINUING STEADFASTLY
IN PRAYER

Romans 12:12

THE LORD IS GOOD TO ALL,
AND HIS TENDER
MERCIES ARE OVER
ALL HIS WORKS.

Psalm 145:9

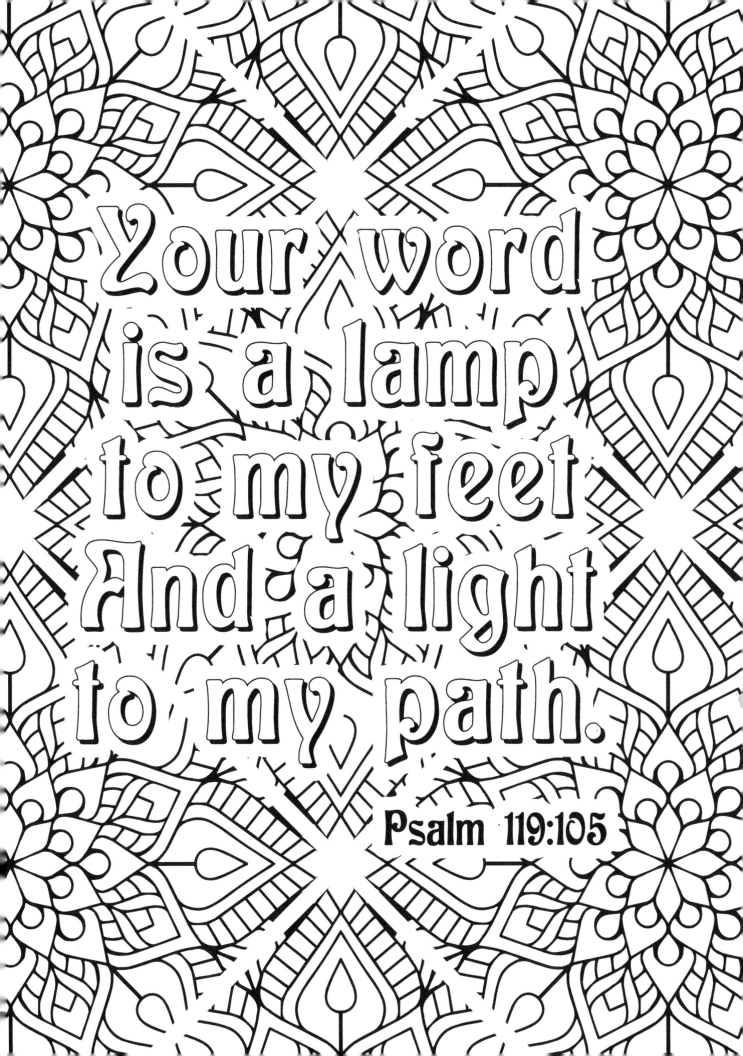

The Lord is my light and my salvation, whom shall I fear?

PSALM 27:1

This is the day
the Lord has made;
We will rejoice and be glad in it.

Psalm 118:24

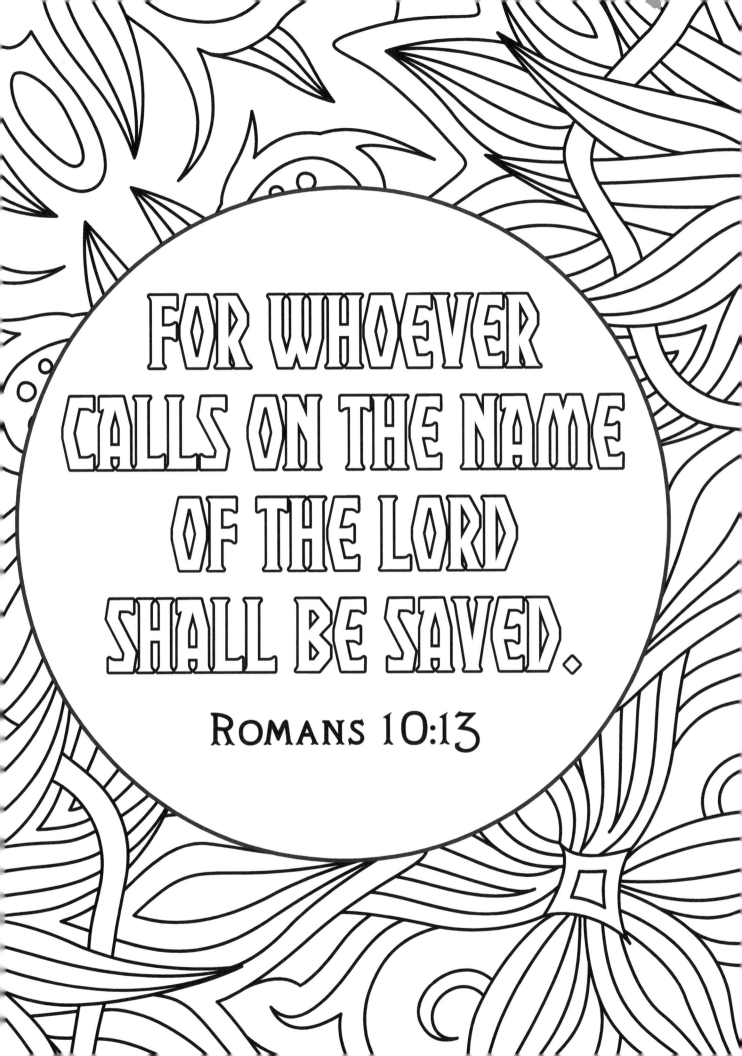

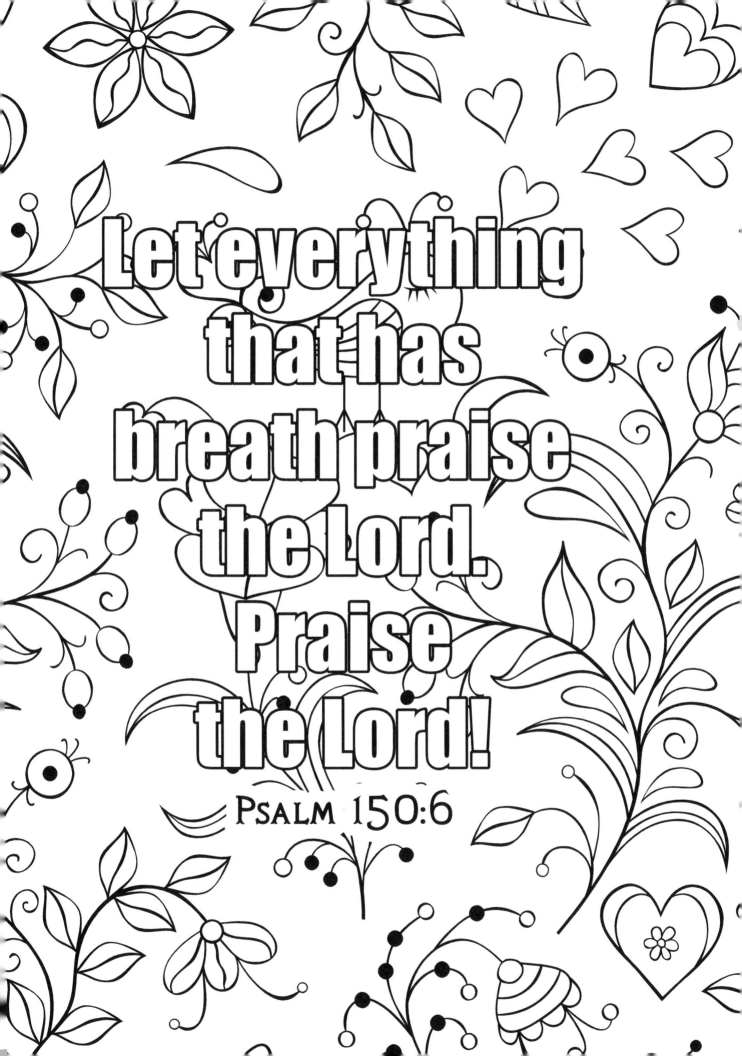

Printed in the USA
CPSIA information can be obtained
at www.ICGtesting.com
LVHW062136281124
797908LV00039B/1574